Angel Tongues & Lobster Tails

Angel Tongues & Lobster Tails

Poems by
MINERVA NEIDITZ

DRYAD PRESS
Washington, D.C. and San Francisco

Copyright © 1999 Dryad Press
All rights reserved under International and Pan-American Copyright Conventions.

Acknowledgments

"Envy" won honorable mention in the 1990 Chester H. Jones Poetry Competition and was produced in their publication; it also appeared in Marilyn Yalom's *A History of the Breast*, Basic Books: 1997. "A First Date" won honorable mention in the 1997 Sandstar Competition and was published in *Visions of Love*, Rockport Press: 1997. "On Route 6 near Provincetown" appeared in *The Cape Codder*, April 1998. "Reunion in Eilat," "Survival," "Wallowing in Winter" and "Raw Foods" appeared in a Charter Oak Cultural Center chapbook, 1998. "How Do You Want to Be Buried? Where Do You Want to Go?" was published as a one-page play in *Lamia Ink!*

Book and cover design by Sandy Rodgers

Cover art: photograph of angel by Minerva Neiditz; photograph of lobster by Robert Bayer, The Lobster Institute.

Published in the United States by
Dryad Press
15 Sherman Avenue
Takoma Park, Maryland 20912

Library of Congress Cataloging-in-Publication Data
Neiditz, Minerva Heller, 1932-
    Angel tongues and lobster tails / by Minerva Neiditz.
   p. cm.
  ISBN 1-928755-01-1
  I. Title.
  PS3564.E29 A84 1999
  811' .54--dc21

Contents

"Man is neither angel nor beast"

Half Angel / 3
A Tarot Card about Lobsters and Mountains / 4
Finding the Beast / 5
God Speaks to Me in Grapefruit / 6
Letting Go / 7
To Rilke / 8
Lost Heroes / 10
The Talisman / 11
Bas-Relief / 12
Grammatical Correctness / 13
Buddha: Call Home / 14
An Endless Search / 15
A Hot Country Moth / 16
Collusion with a Cool Country / 17
The Lord Is My Dentist / 18
The Promised Land / 19
Dying Faultless / 20

"He who would act the angel becomes the beast"

The Muck of Madness / 23
Plea Bargaining / 24
Fearing Success / 25
Envy / 26
Daddy's Little Girl / 27
Call Me Cleopatra / 28
Sugarless / 29
Can't Help It / 30
A First Date / 31
Eclipsed / 32
The Paradox / 33
Splits / 34

Chicken / 35
The Mind, the Body and the Sumo Wrestlers / 36
Couples and Singles / 38
Leaving the House in Dying Condition / 39

"The beast residing at the center of the labyrinth is also an angel"

A Spa Death Wish / 43
A Life Wish / 44
Mother's Milk / 45
Reunion in Eilat / 46
Just Enough / 47
A Paradoxical Relationship / 49
Digging / 51
Raw Foods / 52
Cleaning the Body Electric / 54
Healing / 56
Near His House / 57
On Route 6 Near Provincetown / 58
Figures of Disorder / 59
Wallowing in Winter / 62
White Writing / 63
How Do You Want To Be Buried? Where Do You Want To Go? / 65

With Gratitude

The following friends helped me prepare this book by critiquing and applauding what they read. I've accepted many of their suggestions: Merrill Leffler, Joan Joffe Hall, Matt Proser, Barbara Rosen, C.O. Bennett, Leo Connellan, James Ponet, Elana Ponet, Sue Ellen Thompson, Alice Delana, Marilyn Yalom, Ed Fairstein, Jack Calkins and the poets with whom I studied briefly in the last ten years (Galway Kinnell, Sharon Olds, Carolyn Forche, Anne Waldman and Gerald Stern). I am also grateful to the following places where I've been able to write these poems: The Omega Institute, Rancho La Puerta, and my beloved house in Truro at Cape Cod.

To My Son Robert, Whose Spirit Is Indomitable

*Man Is Neither
Angel Nor Beast*
— Pascal

Finding the Beast

An amaryllis pops through knots in my pine coffin.
My dark spirit rushes outside to find a tiger.

"Who let him out?" I cry in this red riot of spring
when amaryllis pops through knots in the pine coffin.

Orchids bloom in the backyard of a dead marriage.
I tear at the roots of the amaryllis floating like lotus,

lying in a watery lawn of orchids with water seeping
while amaryllis pops through knots in the wooden coffin.

I tear at the roots thrusting through the knotty coffin,
tear and weep, tear and weep for the living dead.

I wake to the power in the stalking tiger.
I wake to the beast I am but cannot kiss.

God Speaks to Me in Grapefruit

In heaven I will never give you half a grapefruit —
I will give you only the whole.
You will suddenly discover
while eating a casserole of cream of wheat
a round orb
as yellow as your soul.

And the oranges will be orange
unshellacked
and the gelatinous core of the grape
will dissolve on your tongue like a wafer
and the bananas, ohhh, the bananas
will hang numinous, voluminous

ready to be stripped.

Letting Go

He wore Old Spice and tweeds,
tried to be good, "Not a whore,"
he whispered in his sleep.
He hated things seeping out
and toothpaste caps lying idle.
He wanted to stay smaller than his father,
but they both loved the rich and famous.
He dropped names and his underwear on the floor,
put lights out continually,
grew hard deposits in his arms,
and puffy veins throughout his body,
gave me radios for birthdays,
read four newspapers a day,
dropped clippings on my breakfast plate,
as if I were a depository.
The speed with which he ate was alarming.

Nevertheless, he was charming,
giving wine to every hostess and his influence.
Underneath his clothes there was less and less to see.
Sometimes his nose resembled a banana and his hair kinked.
His mother came to straighten it with hot oil.
Once I heard him wonder what it would be like
to live at the Cape and catch bluefish.

I wish he were here.
I wish I'd been clearer about his needs.
I wish I had understood how cigarettes and booze made him feel.
I wish he hadn't left me alone, died in the street in winter.
I wish I could have stopped his teeth from grinding.
I wish I could mind my own business and leave him
in some heavenly hotel playing chess with his cronies.

To Rilke

Wasn't it summer when we met?
— the summer when I wrote about flowers and trees
and the leaves filling with light, sharp-edged
and pure like maidens.

Yes, it was summer
and I thought I would never forget you
because we sang the same songs,
belonged to fathers whom we tricked with perfect report cards.

Both of us had promising voices,
but you were in touch with the size of fruit,
and its smooth, unmottled skin and sonnets and angels.

And I was more attuned to motion
and the rhythm of bellies and breasts.

"Drink to me only with thine eyes,"
you kept sighing
and I drank but was still thirsty
for kisses in places you could
not see.

How much I wished you would go fishing in me,
golden, glistening and free from the worries of time and death,
those distractions.... "If I ever die," I said.
"Of course you're going to die," you answered,

you, with your immortal verses,
dismissed my one illusion.... Yes.
It was summer,
but not a fated one,
as you lay in my arms, feeling —

You repaid me with a rough reminder
that I would fade like a rose,
that I should seize the day before
grey touched my locks.

Fie upon you, poet of the ideal,
I am real, wrinkled and ripe for
lusty love. My impulse comes
from below, not above.

It fits me truer
than your praise
of my eyebrow.

Lost Heroes

When we used to take the ferry to the Vineyard,
I watched
so the babies wouldn't fall
into the foam

and you were smoking and reading
the *New York Times*
and I was staring at the Compound
dreaming about future presidents.

That was before you died
and left me trying to understand
the mad world
with a terrified mind,
watching each hero
fall through the rails
into dark waters.

The Talisman

Mothers beat their breasts
when they hear the bronchial rattle in a son's chest.
"Guilty," screams the voice within,

"You should have, could have left him home
on the range, safe in a box with teddy bear,
with cowboy boots and Indian feathers."

You must ward off disaster
with a box of animal crackers —
anything to help him feel your nearness.

If it's father protecting son,
son will carry a shrunken skull.
A symbol of the enemy in parchment.

Grown-ups grow out of protections,
become our own rain coat,
pull up our bridges and moats.

Rattle our rain sticks blue
till the heavens open.
We watch a lucky horseshoe.

It bends in the fire.
We fit the calks
to an adult desire.

Bas-Relief

It was a relief when you died.
I cried, of course,
but I knew you had suffered enough.
You said, "I have to love you.
You're my daughter."
That slip of a tongue
tipped me into darkness.

I feel your hands in the tub,
rub-a-dub dub.
You left me in my crib reeking.
When daddy pasted stars on my
report cards, you said,
"You read too much."
I paid for his love
with your resentment
and now, no matter what I achieve, I grieve....

Grammatical Correctness

I'll tell you something you won't forget.
When my father dried up in that period of chemo
and you were drinking two pints a day,
you both smelled like rotting flesh,
covered with flies.

His lips cracked when he smiled;
his eyes caressed with diminishing light.
Your lips bled vodka; your skin
was as yellow as piss;
you both smelled
like rotting flesh smothered in flies.

I've tried the grammar of yoga, the structure
of T'ai Chi,
and when I'm centered
and silent,
words radiate numinously,
but I'll tell you something I can't forget,
— the stench of your rotting flesh.

I still see his lips like clay,
your lips decaying with vodka.
I smell you both night after night,
two dying animals lying
under a column of flies.

Buddha: Call Home

What would Buddha's mother say on Mother's Day
if he forgot to call?
Would she have been appalled?
Or would she think he had turned to drink?
Would she have worried about him
sitting so long under that tree?
Would she have understood why he renounced her,
as sons must do if they are saints?

Paintings don't show Jesus worshipping Mary after he's grown.
She just weeps at his feet, as mothers do when fate thrusts
their sons upward.

Better to have borne simpletons who win Wimbledons,
who stay nearby, don't fly so high,
but call on Mother's Day.

An Endless Search

I am coming out of a trance
of waiting to be chosen, to be taken in
by mothers, fathers, husbands, presidents.

All of us children, like kittens
losing our mittens, playing inside,
fearing the coming out,

out of the clam shell,
out of the conch or cockle,
out of the shelter, into the world,

where we can be eaten as food for worms.
I have lived dreaming my husband can't die,
my thoughts will preserve my aging parents.

I dream of collecting insurance claims
on premiums I've paid for automobiles and houses.
I've bought stock and municipal bonds

to keep me safe from tragic consequences,
or the inevitable laws of change, gravity, decay.
What can I say now, finally,

after this endless search for protection,
but thank you, thank you
for leaving me my teeth.

A Hot Country Moth

When will I feel the sorrow
of my search for love,
the habitual ritual
of opening to the new,
curious about "you,"
living like a moth,
slothfully flying,
touching in French,
tatonner, tatonner, tatonner,
orbiting blindly,
losing its way,
looking for light
that resembles a source,
cool enough to alter
its course to a middle
and ending,
instead of spiraling round the same
petty 60 watts,
as common as a hot country,
or dreams of eternal incandescence?

Collusion With a Cool Country

You are an Anglo-Saxon male
of English descent,
not especially bright,
but at night you grow beans
and climb up the stalk
to the land of corporate giants.

Fee! Fi! Fo!
You are looking for dough,
expecting me to give you
the chicken, not the soup,
a foxy capitalist
in the hen house.

I never liked the obvious.
I won't hide you under
my skirt, or play that
oedipal trick,
so you can stick
it to the jolly green father.

The Lord Is My Dentist

The lord is my dentist.
I shall not want.
He fills my cavities,
restores my enamel,
leads me down, down
into a dreamless sleep,
where he clasps me like a Spanish dancer.
I droop in his powerful embrace.
He tells me stories about his alcoholic father
who left his mother
who saw him now and then,
which is why he is a dentist,
in order to be painless.
He can mix chemicals deftly
with the pestle of his pinkie,
come in at an angle,
to clamp and thrust in his quivering drill.

Yea though I let him enter the mysteries of my mouth,
his touch comforts me.
I lie in the incline of his leather chair forever,
till I am polished, pure and plaqueless.
My rinsing cup runneth over.

The Promised Land

I survived my life in the desert solo,
brought treasures up from my depths like Marco Polo,
ventured beyond this tiny village of rock throwers,
laughed a lot when they worshipped their golden calves.

You, on the other hand, played games well.
No one knew your secrets; no one caught you
sucking a call girl's toes.
You could carry the Torah, climb mountains, accept responsibility.
I wanted to go with you to Canaan,
to cross the River, to see the patriarchal promise,
the olive trees, the sheep grazing, the Sea of Galilee.
I forgot you were human.

You began to wonder what life might be
in that land you sought but couldn't imagine.
"What will you feed me? You know I can't eat fish.
Here, at least, there's manna. Will there be knish in Canaan?

Will you still be faithful when I'm eighty-three?
Will you wash the dishes and cuddle-coddle me?"
Oh Moses, Moses, you will never be free.
You always want some signed guarantee.

You love those tablets of stone.
What we know is bone to bone.
Your days are more numbered than mine — perhaps.
You're already having memory lapses.

You may have to eat what appears on your plate
if it doesn't wiggle.
Can't you start to giggle?
Otherwise, I know a man called Joshua.

Dying Faultless

When you visited the Dead Sea
you spoke to a life guard and found
that many tourists had drowned.
"They were all old," he said.
"They float on their bellies," he said,
Their neck muscles were weak.
They could not lift their heads.

We squirmed uncomfortably at the image
of old people drowning
in a sea of salt.
But I've thought about it
since we last spoke
and I've concluded that we joked about
a new way of dying faultless,

not becoming a pillar of salt,
because of backward glances,
but rolling over
as in a bed,
to sleep in a sea
reserved for the dead.

*He Who Would Act the Angel
Becomes the Beast*
— Pascal

The Muck of Madness

You who romanticize madness
should live with it forever
should feel fixed in kindergarten
swing back and forth
in the same room
with the same teacher
stuck in her play dough
and your stray thoughts.

Plea Bargaining

You didn't pay attention
when Cain brought his offering.
He was a soil tiller, not a sheep killer,
probably a vegetarian.

Of course, his face fell
when You chose Abel's lamb.
Nobody wants to be second best,
but he didn't try harder.

Instead he killed his brother.
That wasn't the right response,
an overreaction to Your rejection,
and then You banished him.

You were merciful, I suppose,
when You marked his forehead;
yet the land of Nod, east of Eden,
hasn't taught us much.

Perhaps You could rethink Your solution?

Fearing Success

When we all spoke the same language,
You were worried.
"There'll be no stopping them,"
You thought,
as we built the shining tower and the city on the hill.

You confounded our speech,
scattered us everywhere like pigeons.

Why couldn't YOU handle just a little competition?

Envy

Melanie Klein said
that little children
are envious of their mother's breasts
and imagine that they can enter them
and scoop out all their goodness.

If what she says is true,
few of us would ever
suckle such savages.

Yet it does explain original sin,
and how I avoid empty refrigerators,
and why I never let you touch my scars.

Daddy's Little Girl

Before I die I'm going back to the candy store, daddy,
where you'll open your wallet and I'll take all you've got,
buy sweets for the journey, pink and green mints,
and juicy fruits, non-pareils and butter creams,
as varied as the dreams I've had of you,
my loving man with the dancing eyes,
who kept me from other men who
couldn't give the way you gave,
daddy, opening your wallet
wide and feeding me
nothing but sweets.

Call Me Cleopatra

Call me Cleopatra,
Queen of Denial,
admire my throat,
the skin that flutes from a chin
refusing to double its bloat.

At sixty I doze in my boat,
with some old goat gasping,
pleading for favors,
the flavors of my scents,
drowned in the quivering movement

of my asp, crawling
to prick the point on my breast
where Antony lay his head,
thinking that I was dead,
when I was only resting.

Sugarless

When the lovemaking stops,
my belly rumbles.
You mix cornmeal and eggs
like a Navajo, fix bacon and I open
a can of soup.

Now your kitchen drama begins.
"I hate to cook," you growl,
but you won't let me take over.

Now we're back in the land of Giants.
You are mother showing father

how perfect the corn cakes can be.
Now you are father complaining
that the cakes aren't good enough.
You are frozen in her dream of resentment,
cooking for someone who cannot love.

Now we become four
and I marvel at the way
we had been one,
and how that one
got lost in a pan.

"Please, don't put sugar in the batter," I ask
"Remember, I'm diabetic."
"I'm following the recipe," you bark.
I hear your "have-to."
You will never hear my plea.

You can only follow a recipe, a recipe, a recipe.

Can't Help It

Who would have guessed you were the god I had sought,
slightly shorter and mostly thin,
wearing green polyester and a red baseball
hat — a gestalt therapist doing schizo-
phrenia research, standing at the railroad station
holding a red tulip in your hands,
though once we started to talk, externals faded.

You were the voice lifting the seven veils,
awakening me from slumber, putting me back
to sleep with Yiddish lullabies, creating
a multi-media event inside me,
acting as though our parents came from the same
shtetl, understanding my sorrows and joys.

When we finally kissed,
every bird broke its throat,
the peacock crying to the cuckoo,
the nightingale blending its ballad
with the swoon of the mourning dove.

O My Love, you have lingered long,
but now I can fall again, falling in love again,
fall once again in love.

A First Date

His earliest memory was
of swinging in the hammock with his brother
looking up at the sky through the leaves
and how his mother came with two bowls:
one of strawberries
one with sour cream
and sweat was pouring down her throat into her cleavage
and he, a four year old,
offered her his berries
and she said,"Eat, eat, they're for you."

That's what he remembers,
along with the nazis
killing her and his father and his brother
killing them all,
killing them all.

My first memory is wandering
in the streets of New York alone,
lost at the age of two, thinking that my house
must be near,
not understanding the fear of distances.
This trip was like walks to the butcher shop.
Familiarity should be right around the corner.

And now we meet
for the first time in this strange New York town.
We've both been down, down,
and come back up again
to taste the strawberries with cream,
the sour and the sweet
of those we've lost
and the promise of finding them again.

Eclipsed

Watching the cold black mother cloud
cover the moon,
I refuse to merge
join the crowd
or lose my skin.

The stones glow
as I walk around a granite labyrinth
remembering the sunflowers
nodding and sleeping
waiting for the dawn.

The stars as animals or men
no longer speak to me.
All reflection is illusion,
like the shining
of cleomes or peonies or poppies

ecstatically bobbing as though
light dwells within.

The message comes, "Wait
wait until morning
when you will open your eyes."

But what if there is no sunshine
to bring me back from
this cold kingdom of stones,
separate and alone,
this shrouded night without imagination?

The Paradox

The limitless dwells outside my window;
sometimes I let her in.
She is a blonde child wanting everything,
a wilderness drawing me into her landscape.

Should I shut the window on her fingers
and make her fall into the void?

I look in the mirror at my breakfast face.
My hands portion out each sun-dried grape.
I measure this or that, tat or tit.
I am a shoe looking for a foot to fit.

It's best when I feel rooted and brown,
like an olive tree, gnarled and dry; my branches
reach no higher than a man and I know who
I am and what I'm supposed to do.

Then I can welcome the pleasures of each day,
Knowing the lost ideal for which I've paid.

Splits

The golden seal at the Boston aquarium
lies between two parents
with ear slits opening to city sounds
and the slush of playing waters.

His tail divides in duality;
I imitate his arch.
I cannot touch my other pole
or bounce on cold concrete.

But I have skills he doesn't have;
so my revenge is sweet —
these words that show I can talk,
these walking, patterned feet.

Chicken

You stood in the poulet store where diners in a rush
could grab cooked carrots and pommes frites;
you looked like a large brown thrush,
a bird talking to herself.

Nothing prepared me for the woman who said,
"I know you. Didn't we take Great Books together?"
"Yes, I remember. You always asked why....
not like the others who watched Lear die and said nothing."

"Do you wake up wanting to live?" you asked
and then you mauled me with the tale of your three efforts to die;
you wanted me to cry for your husband who still lived
 — a vegetable — you had to divorce him to cancel his debts.
Your sons had abandoned you — your friends as well.

What was I to say to someone who had been so fortunate?
I understand. I've been there too. You must stop this anger
against yourself. You must smile on the streets of this cold,
inhumane city where no one has time.

"Have you tried working or going back to school?" I asked.
If anything, you looked bleaker than before.
I grabbed my chicken and fled to the door
hoping not to see your name in the obituaries.

The Mind, the Body and the Sumo Wrestlers

It's been raining and I'm dreaming
about two round sumo wrestlers
dressed in regal gold and apple green brocades

It's been raining and I'm trusting
that my own ark will float
when the fountains of the deep burst apart

It's been raining and I'm coughing
with beasts of every kind
cooped up and pissing to mark their terrain

It's been raining and I'm watching
those round sumo wrestlers
with their store of hara power below the waist

They channel energy
up the spine, up the chakras, up
to the centers of awareness,

as if they were red at the root
then orange in the belly
then yellow above the naval

and at the heart
there is green for balance.
Green is the color of

balance when the heart opens
when you're on your way,
your right Wu Li Way

and you finally open
the window for fresh air
and the dove flies forth and it returns.

Couples and Singles

It's been raining and I've been wondering about weather
and how I mimicked Lena Horne with an umbrella
singing, "Just can't get my poor old self
together," in the fourth grade
and how my father
bulged with pride and mother cried, afraid
I loved a black singer more than her.

It's been raining and I'm tossing out the contents
of my attic: paintings, silver, diplomas,
baby clothes, teething rings, books
I'll never read and poems I wrote long
ago, long ago.

It's been raining and I'm living in my ark,
my body and
I'm ready for more rain,
full of feisty poetry and beasts of every kind.

They are coupled like doves, like doberman pinschers,
but some have lost their significant others.

We write verses and the ark floats on a sea
of sharks
and we pray for the mist to rise and the sun
to shine
on Christian and Jew, Muslim and Buddhist,
lover and stranger.

Finally, we embrace, and the waters recede
and the dry land appears
with a rainbow arching across the sky
and the dove flies forth
and it returns.

Leaving the House in Dying Condition

As I
   die
I'll be paying bills
leaving frozen dinners
   for
         all the Hungry Men
        who didn't come to say
"Goodbye."

Only Grisette
will
   water the plants
         and weep
at my feet
     while I sleep
dreaming,

perhaps I might
         meet someone   who'll bless me
      for being strong enough
to
    live and
die   without him.

*The Beast Residing
at the Center of the Labyrinth
Is Also an Angel*

— Thomas More

A Spa Death Wish

I want to die in an herbal wrap.
I want my body to drain
into that rubbery cloth,
my skin to soak in the broth
of rosemary, lavender and thyme
like a wild ambrosial swan
stuffed and basted,
tasted by the heavenly hosts
singing thanks for the gift of me.

A Life Wish

Lead me from the dead callous
to the live blood in my toes,
from the false steps on a dark trail
to the turbulent ocean teeming
with bluefish and shark.

I could be a grain of sand
joining others to rise
like a castle where the king sits
with his queen stroking her golden hair.

They sit on a throne of honor
and govern an invisible kingdom.
She touches his dry wounds;
his flesh fills with flowers.
He touches her womb;
she composes music with light.

Mother's Milk

For me the excitement comes
from a boy at my breast sucking,
when I hold a son in my arms
as I proffer milk
and his lips pounce on the nipple
and squeeze my nerves
straight down to the uterus.

He drinks me in
with closed eyes,
as we drown in a sea of caresses —
his fingers touching lightly
like my thoughts.

Year after year little boys come,
writers and teachers,
blondes and redheads,
belonging to others,
they come into my attic dreams to play
and always and always,
they lie down to suck.

At last, letting go of the young,
I find newcomers invading,
tall, bearded, wrinkled and alien.

Where are their passports?
I need registrations before I can welcome them.
This is, of course, a proper European hotel.
I know they belong,
but somehow they feel like strangers,
and I doubt if they drink milk.

Reunion in Eilat

I've met you again in Eilat
where it is so hot it's hard to breathe.
Ambition leaves my brain.
I turn toward loss and pain to weave
a dream in which we sit upon blue cloth.

Do you remember a widow named Wroth
with two daughters,
one with a hump
from a heart that needed jump-starting at birth?

In my dream we part again and again,
but this time you are glad I know
which seeds grow in sandy soil,
how to toil until poems sprout,
like this wondrous pink Eilat, a spotless place,
where those who cannot find
their lost loves come
to lie in the sun and ponder
why some are born with injured hearts,
while others will acquire them.

Just Enough

I.

Just enough snow has fallen,
just enough to cover the scars,
the gnarling branches,
to silence the dogs,
to help me pass into bird form
searching for seeds.

II.

Memory takes me down, down on a sled
under the body of a boy pressing his pea-
jacketed penis against my spine,
until a question in my five-year-old-
mind rises:
"Is this the puppy dog
tail little boys are made of?"

When he comes for cocoa, I wear red.
"You look pretty," he says, kissing me on the nose.
I show him my toes,
particularly the one stunted by a machine
that showed the skeleton in a shoe.
He doesn't seem to mind,
proving that five-year-old love is blind.
I wish I could find him again, but instead,
I meet men dreaming images of perfection, ideal blonde bodies.

III.

Richard tells me I'm fat
when I complain about his drinking.
Am I loving him too little or too much?
I loved William too much,
the man who loved winter,

I tried to climb his mountains,
only to fall,
tear ligaments and scar my knees,
humiliated by his teasing.
But I saw his snips and snails,
the other male parts he was made of,
and he tasted my sugar and an infinite variety of spice.

IV.

I'm sorry I am not a wife,
but I rather like this new curriculum,
not loving too little or too much,
learning to love just enough,
to cover the scars,
to silence the dogs,
to leave my imperfect claw prints in the snow.

A Paradoxical Relationship

Not father, not brother,
not God in male drag,
not earth-mother-goddess,
not lover from my own darkness,
not sister, not innocent virgin,
walking the streets of Paris at midnight.

Let none of these speak to me now;
but rather some other creature
from an unknown denomination.
Not scientist, not robot from outer space,
not a construct from the cold wars,
nor a blonde surfer breaking with the sea upon the shore.

No! my next love will be beyond complements
of two groping toward a whole apple.
My next lover will be whole.
A male-female-father-mother-sister-brother-
innocent-experienced angel-beast,
not limited to genitalia.
Not the opposition of multiple orgasms
to one measly erection!

My next lover will contain the container,
and the container will contain a gaping mouth
and multiple tongues that speak indiscriminately
to toes and nose and lips.

BE MINE, I'll call you,
who will not settle for one orifice,
one dark abyss that breeds claustrophobia.
S/he will play voraciously,
cleaning like a cat,

as I sit in my autonomous car.
I'll watch the soapy strokes through closed windows
until it's time for green thoughts and fresh air,
and then, only then, will we breathe
as I have never breathed before
and perhaps it will feel like death.

The notes in our cells will play lullabies
and we will speak in rhythms
and the mania of expectations will disappear
and disappointment will reveal:

You did not lead me into green pastures
You did not guard me like a sheep
You did not restore my soul
You did not ration me correctly.

Instead, You gave me a few transient moments
to breathe Your breath
within my breath.

So now I go beyond these clichés
of plenty and paradise
to a place where there are fewer lies,
where the not-so-beautiful you and the not-so-beautiful I
rise through whispers and kisses, rise through singing and sighs.

Digging

I met a woman who's eighty-seven
who weeds her garden at dawn
and buys cars with large back seats
for the wheel chairs of her friends
and spends her days helping them replace their glasses or teeth.

And I wished as I had never wished before
that I might be like her,
oblivious of myself.

Her parents died when she was only eight
and she traveled alone
from New Mexico to Colorado
and married
and lost two sons
and a husband to boot.

How different the digging for a better rooted-word,
weeding a verbal garden at first light!

Raw Foods

My mother knew more
than my father;
she ate avocados.

Untutored in higher discourse,
she spoke words
like "gornischt helfen."

"Gornischt helfen,"
You can't help it,
mama said.

That would release all shame
and guilt, the waste
polluting my brain.

I'd scrape my knees;
I'd lose my purse.
"Gornischt helfen."

Daddy read Emanuel Kant,
pure Reason,
He smoked cigarettes;

He drank beer
and died at seventy-two.
"Gornischt helfen."

Mama lived
to be eighty-three,
thanks to God.

He was a Guide;
he was a teacher,
a deep attachment.

Yet mama keeps me
alive today
on sprouts and avocados.

Cleaning the Body Electric

> In meditation our bodies burn the dross of
> impurity. Our task is to accelerate that process.
> to become the light we were and will be again.
>
> > Pir Vilayat Kahn, leader of the Sufis

I.

"Cleanliness is next to Godliness," my mother said
restoring maidenhead to everything sullied and begrimed.
She never exercised or read books on the meaning of the sublime.

I still hire "cleaning people" to wash
baseboards, dirty boots, and crusted pots,
but I change the linens and scrub my jogging suits.

I also teach unruly students to write —
which feels remote from the bending of aging knees,
the bubbly shampooing, removing stains and spots.

II.

Dark as obsidian, some inner cleaning force
washes my intestinal wall, dark because
it knows the magic from some unconscious source.

It performs rituals with attention, knows what to flush
and save — and, of course, knows other mental mysteries
like eliminating deadwood from a poem.

III.

On the subject of cleaning auras, I've watched a healer
howl into the back of a live body,
then suck out the interfering blue

or grey dead light that should be white.
I've watched her push and pull away, stop
and pray over someone needing to rise

out of a negative, vibrational disguise.
So that is why I can ask you,
my skeptical friend, "What if you were light?

What if you were born clean? What if you
were not meant to become ignoble and mean?

What if? What if we had a pair of wings?
If Whitman were right when he sang of the body electric?"

Healing

Our minds are measurable in waves.
Each has its name:
beta or alpha, theta or delta.

Labeling has comforted,
limiting the chaos,
thoughts beyond control.

But even chaos has boundaries.
I should not feel
your mess as mess.

It may be a higher form
of paradox between yin and yang,
randomly rigid, predictably chancy.

Healing feels like delta beige,
not beta red or alpha yellow,
or "Eureka I've found it" purple.

Healing flows beyond comprehension,
a potpouri of balanced sounds and scents,
from the place within where we are music and flowers.

Sometimes the earth looks flat,
especially when the music stops
in our cellular walls.

Suddenly you can hear a high-pitched sound
calling you home and your neurons begin to flow
into a deep valley to mingle like rabbits.

Then they produce some round simple answers
to the jumble of fantasies wishing to be born.

Near His House

In Paris the delphinia grow tall;
they are the princes at the ball;
they remind the forget-me-nots
to not forget about lovers;
they force the poppies and peonies to blush;
they make us hush to hear the song
of bluebirds and thrushes.

On Route Six Near Provincetown

Dunes lie exhausted from visitors coming and going,
gobbling lobsters under a yellow moon.
Soon the land must receive into its crooked sleeve
the hordes of huns licking mango sorbet,
eager to pay to lay their bones down for just one day.

But suddenly, as if to say, "Enough!"
a wind starts blowing the mist away.
Dwarf pines and bushes sway;
the wind whips darkly across the sky.
Storm clouds hover as beaches recover
from man, while sand settles in a single, trackless fan.

Figures of Disorder

Test *I*

A.

Was it a test when he asked me to marry him?
I had grown fond of his sharp, angel tongue,
his red, lobster carapace, his bones.

His children shouted a month later, "You're a monster,"
How can you marry with your wife in the earth less than a year?"
They played Hamlet to my evil Claudius.

He suddenly reversed his song, felt he had acted
precipitously, but "Nothing has changed, nothing
has changed, only the fact that I cannot marry."

"Do you still love me?" I whispered,
seeking something to haul me back
from this fishy falling out of an engagement.

"Love is a transitory emotion," he said,
  from some hollow in his chest or in his head.
  I wished him dead.

I jumped out of our bed and fled.
"OUT OF CONTROL," he yelled,
"YOU'RE OUT OF CONTROL."

B.

"The bastard said he couldn't tame me."
I told Matt who said, "That's a compliment.
Why would he want to?"

But now I understand.
He wants a house cat
that never runs through the streets.

C.

Wee Willie Winkie ran through the town
upstairs and downstairs in his nightgown.
I wish I could do that too. Let go
of all laws and principles and shout,
"You HYPOCRITE! You JUDAS! You BETRAYER!

TEST 2

Compare and contrast Richard III and Falstaff as figures
of disorder in their respective plays.
Differentiate between (a) the nature of each
figure's disorder and (b) what or whom his disorder influences.

ANSWER

Richard III had a tight agenda that night
when he murdered the boys in the Tower,
then took wives fresh
from the flesh of dead husbands
he had slaughtered.
He spilled blood as though it were water.

Whereas Falstaff was unruly, loveable,
a soul without a goal.
He simply liked to play night and day

booze and snooze,
read newspapers cover to cover.
He was a lover.
But I don't remember his Mrs.
He received kisses and
died of a broken heart.

B.

"A" says Matt, my friend,
and so ends this tale
of a woman who
loved a lobster
by mistake.

Wallowing in Winter

I am torn between snow and bird song,
not quite ready to sprout into tepid light.

I dream about someone spraying my house with teflon.
I dream about a place in the sky where souls reside
in honeycombs like bees, building sweetness of singularity.

This has been a winter of demi-darkness, surrounded by igloo ice.
No one calls or comes to tea and whenever I go out,
I start to say a prayer;
each time I eat an animal,
I mumble another prayer: •∞§¶ †¥ß∂∫˜◊

I thought that love should bring us closer, but that's wrong.
It is the fear of freezing that clears our eyes,
promotes equality,
mothers our wish to belong.

I wish I had a human family huddled together,
sleeping through endless storms,
smiling in earthy, fecund surroundings.

White Writing

When we were going to marry,
I could kiss you, baby, and carry
you into my brain which worked
like a plain paper fax,
receiving, receiving your words,
holding them as the crystal vase
from Prague
on my piano holds
one chalk-white lily
trembling, while a fogged-over
ancient sea washes you
silently to my shore,
your salty sperm spewing,
unlike the black ink of the ageless squid,
imprinting my glistening sands
with white messages.

Aaaaaah! Blessed writing.

How simple it seemed to read you then!
But now the ten thousand things have appeared:
the tons of solid waste,
your unhappy daughters,
my disabled son,
your extra years,
my fear of becoming subservient,
losing all I've gained
in years of celibacy,
and you, reluctant to use the phone
to call a woman too strong,

a passionate poet longing
for bliss, who kissed you
into a world unknown.

I feel the unexpected frost that comes
too soon
and white
now gleams like snow instead of writing.

How Do You Want To Be Buried?
Where Do You Want to Go?

Scene I

Speaker #1: "My husband says he wants to be buried with his credit cards."

Speaker #2: "I want to be freeze-dried."

Speaker #3: "I'd like a raucous funeral
with games
and sweet meats."

Narrator: Will the living grieve?
There's always time to mourn.
Isn't it better to feel the warmth of friends
after death's cold touch?

Speaker #1: "I especially liked my first wake
a child of three... died of croup....
They laid him out in his lederhosen.
The father wept and the mother smiled
to think he was with the angels,
and now, thirty years later,
she prays to him to help
her find a parking space."

Speaker#2: "That's o.k. as long as she believes it."

Speaker#3: "I don't know what I believe."

Speaker#1: "Then you're like most of us.
You try on new ideas every day."

Narrator: I went to a workshop
once on the "swift and secret path —
how to reach the highest level
of consciousness before death,"
and we chanted "om tara, tu tara,
tureh swa ha,"
and visualized our breath moving up
the chakras to the heart
where we pushed it like a pinball
with an exhalation "POWH"
AND IT PASSED OUT THE TOP OF OUR HEADS
TO AN AMITABBAH BUDDHA
SITTING IN SPACE ON A LILY PAD
and I said to the rinpoche
smiling from ear to ear,
"I don't want to go the the PURE LAND;
I won't know anyone there."
And he replied laughing,
"Don't you know
you'll be without form?"

And then I knew what I would miss,
the smell of rosemary, the taste of papaya and pear,
and the sight of people like you with me
in this sensory world.

Notes

"Lobsters and Mountains." There is a Tarot card which shows a moon, a mountain and a lobster coming out of a stream.

"To Rilke." Rilke sang a great many songs about fruit and angels and the disembodied spirit.

"The Talisman." Anne Waldman asked poets in her workshop to bring an object which they carried with them on their journeys. One man brought in a shrunken skull.

"Collusion with a Cool Country." Robert Bly states in his tape on "fairy tales" that men usually have to find a woman in the ranks of a corporation to help them climb up the ladder, to show them the ropes.

"Eclipsed." There is a labyrinthine garden at the Omega Institute in Rhinebeck, New York, where I witnessed this eclipse.

"A Life Wish." Robert Bly and Marion Woodman taught a workshop together in Toronto on the subject of creativity. I had never before seen a man and woman share the stage equally, with mutual respect.

"Reunion in Eilat." As Louise Glück says in "A Fantasy," "It's her only hope, the wish to move backward/ And just a little, not so far as the marriage, but the first kiss."

"A Paradoxical Relationship." Sharon Olds challenges you to astound her. This was my response. It astounded me.

"Cleaning the Body Electric." In Part III, I'm referring to Barbara Brennan who is a scientist and a healer. She has a school on Long Island where she teaches people to clean auras. I met her at Omega. I did not see an aura. However, I do believe that some proof is available in "Kirlian" photography, which shows a vaporous cloud rising out of the body at the moment of death. A scientist I spoke to believes auras could be infra-red rays emanating from the head. Why not the whole body?

"Wallowing in Winter." Souls do speak in dreams. I found my humorous soul living in a condo in the sky, a nest for a single woman like a cubicle in a honeycomb.

About the Author

Minerva Heller Neiditz likes to think of herself as having nine lives. In 1988 her first book of poetry, *On the Way*, was published by Paper Moon Press in Washington, D.C. where she was born in 1932. This was during her fifth life. Her first life was as a student, culminating in a B.A. from Smith College and an M.A. from Radcliffe. Her second life as the wife of David H. Neiditz, a Connecticut State Senator, included being the mother of two sons, Robert and Jonathan. Her third life as a Ph.D. candidate who specialized in "Banishment: Separation and Loss in the Later Plays of Shakespeare" preceded teaching at Trinity College. In her fourth life she was president of her own company, The Writing Consultants. Her fifth life continues as a poet. Her sixth life was as Director of the Institute of Writing at the University of Connecticut and as an assistant professor of Managerial Communications in the School of Business at UConn.

She has recently retired from her academic career and is now concentrating on writing in her seventh life. In addition to these seven lives, she has been politically active (the first chairperson of the Connecticut Permanent Commission on the Status of Women, an organizer of legislative campaigns and an activist in peace groups such as Women for a Meaningful Summit.

She lives in Hartford, Connecticut and in Truro, Massachusetts, where she spends part of the summer. She hopes to have two more lives before the nine are up.